CW01508428

CLEMENTINES

(A COLLECTION OF POEMS)

by
Orok Otu Duke

Grosvenor House
Publishing Limited

All rights reserved
Copyright © Orok Otu Duke, 2013

Orok Otu Duke is hereby identified as author of this
work in accordance with Section 77 of the Copyright, Designs
and Patents Act 1988

The book cover picture is copyright to Amayo Orok Duke

This book is published by
Grosvenor House Publishing Ltd
28-30 High Street, Guildford, Surrey, GU1 3EL.
www.grosvenorhousepublishing.co.uk

This book is sold subject to the conditions that it shall not, by way of
trade or otherwise, be lent, resold, hired out or otherwise circulated
without the author's or publisher's prior consent in any form of
binding or cover other than that in which it is published and
without a similar condition including this condition being imposed
on the subsequent purchaser.

A CIP record for this book
is available from the British Library

ISBN 978-1-78148-830-0

Contents

An Introduction

I wish I knew all the days

That I would have you my way.

Our liaison acts like the phoenix

In stolen moments that we may fix.

Lightning is the forebear of the thunder,

Your glow allows my storm to plunder.

It is like sucking nectar with every bite

And munching clementines in the night.

This secret pact we have shared

May somehow get us ensnared.

-INFIDELS © Orok Otu Duke (Clementines)

My thoughts, ideas and prejudices are usually vented through safe and legal channels and permissible formats, like prose, poetry, drama and mass media (including new media).

African communities still consider works of art along utilitarian lines. The local audience readily minimises the basic aesthetics of works of art to accommodate the propagandist qualities and values of such works. Therefore, we seek to serve both our immediate communities and the wider society.

My research reveals that: A clementine is a variety of mandarin orange (Citrus reticulata). The exterior is a deep orange colour with a smooth, glossy appearance. Clementines can be separated into seven to fourteen segments. They tend to be very easy to peel, like a tangerine, but are almost always seedless. For this reason, they are sometimes known as seedless tangerines or the Algerian tangerine. They are typically juicy and sweet, with less acid than oranges. Their oils, like other citrus fruits, contain mostly limonene, as well as myrcene, linalool, and many complex aromatics.

Clementines, usually grown in Algeria, Spain, Morocco, Italy, Israel, Lebanon, and Turkey, have been available in Europe and the United States for many years.

My Clementines touches on social, political and philosophical issues discerned from my experience, perception and convictions. For the audience, you are at liberty to also appreciate these poems according to your cosmology, experience and orientation. Proceed, then: analyse, assess, peel it and savour it – if you must.

Orok Otu Duke
London, England.
August, 2012

REFERENCES:

1. Edible: An Illustrated Guide to the World's Food Plants. National Geographic. 2008. p. 73.
2. Ziegler, Herta (2007). Flavourings: production, composition, applications, regulations. John Wiley p.203
3. Harper, Douglas (November 2001). "Clementine". Online Etymology Dictionary. Retrieved February 14, 2009.
4. Saunt, James (January 2000). Citrus Varieties of the World (Second edition). Sinclair International Business Resources. ISBN 978-1-872960-01-2.
5. Hodgson, Richard Willard (1967). : Horticultural Varieties of Citrus. University of California, Division of Agricultural Sciences. Retrieved February 14, 2009.

Dedication

To my wife, Viktoria and our four children:
Orok, Heaven, Amayo and Nikkita.
My family, wherein hibernates my Muse.

-Orok Otu Duke

Crying Time Is Over

It has been going on for too long to even become a lingo,
This relapsed situation has overwhelmed Emeka Aliko,
Who can't feed with his family and is running out of jobs,
Official mobs are unleashed on us the door knobs.

How can you live with all that you have done to us?
Now our fragile hearts have been ripped and torn,
This country belongs to us all, we will never leave,
Or ignore injustice, until real freedom is achieved.

All I now see is scarlet red,
Scores are lying down dead,
This is another killing field,
Same known people, I now can see.

We are economically abused,
Physically and mentally bruised,
The refrain is, "enough is enough",
So know when to stop acting tough.

If you know how to mend the fence,
Then we will have recompense,
Since the mass action exposed the lies,
Cut through red tape before more blood flies.

Innocent blood that is stained on your shirt,
Serves as a reminder of how we feel hurt,
You muffled our cries of anger and grief,
While the whole world watched in disbelief.

Some people wanted you to be gone,
They thought your ascension was very wrong,
I remember how we sang the freedom song,
With activists who were just and not scared,
Insisting on you, as the office was shared.

You now cut us so deep,
The masses' blood begins to seep,
We are the ones now exposed to all the rains,
Ashamed, we now wear a fez cap to hide the pains.

Methinks we were comrades like gum and glue,
With your actions, we are feeling blue,
When the truth finally hits the floor,
To expose fingerprints on the till's door.
We pray that you will have nothing to say,
And hand over the culprits to pay,
This country belongs to us all, we will never leave,
Or ignore injustice, until real freedom is achieved.

Deregulation

We should desist from whining and crying,
Assume our future and start the rallying,
The motive that was immaculate and sublime,
Has an image now not even fit for a swine,
Comrades for elections are now miscreants,
And thugs, while you keep a safe distance.

The citizens are not just buying,
Children and mothers are now dying,
This suffering is really no more edifying.

Swallow your pride now and take the bitter pill,
Do a housecleaning with any one bill,
Deregulate and regulate, just save the national till,
Blind man's bluff was a schoolyard game,
In our country we are no more the same,
Shoving us into economic clouds.

The citizens are not just buying,
Children and mothers are here dying.
This suffering is really no more edify.

All at Once

Your internecine hopes, dreams and desires,
Are clearly reflected in our bodily attires
And you condescend to scatter the
Condiments for assuaging our domestic deity,
All at once.

The roughshod rides we endured were tantamount
To pure hate and disdain, we now understand,
You have become deaf and dumb and unyielding
To entreaties and intercessions from every building,
All at once.

Searing distant ovations that you mistake as a rant,
Were somnolent grumbles moulded into a chant,
The ululations that greeted you and became a cant,
Have translated into seismic waves in the instant,
All at once.

Whenever the lion feeds, something must die,
These tintinnabulations should be reduced to a chime,
Our recent history and struggles are being put to test,
Patriotism and reason will put these sizzles to rest,
All at once.

Your Cabal

You bother about this freedom strike,
When there is putrid religious strife,
Where whimsical, fratricidal attrition
Threatens us as a united nation.

Now your insipid obduracy belies
The official advocacy of bestial lies,
This crossroad unveils governmental putridity,
Boosted by the vocal and visible nonentities.

A documentation of tales reveals horrid atrocities
In Damaturu, filicide, infanticide and matricide in Jos,
Sororicide in Potiskum, and siblicide in Madalla,
Patricide and uxoricide are commonplace,
Now consolidating genocide against the populace.

Your insensitivity is crass irresponsibility,
Your ascension was to be serendipity,
All your advocates now deserve our pity,
Marooned and desolate, we are, over the city.

Our contention was you as divine intervention,
Now transformed into a supine instrumentation.

Hope

Genesis is the cock-crow at dawn,
When the sun unveils an unwitting pawn,
Flexing sinews and muscular brawn,
With shapely birds chirping all along,
Dancing and serenading my song,
In time, i will hear them say,
"All will be well, some day".

We wake to view famished lands in tow,
With events of the day, lined up in rows,
Out of abundance, some sleep so deep,
Due to a lack, some bear grudges to sleep,
A lack of love makes some refuse to sleep
Still, at dusk all hearts remember to say,
"All will be well, some day".

On the farm, the hands toil and get weary,
Fisherman stares into Catfish River stymied,
Sedentary and sentry life, the soul is rallied,
The farmer is looking on, so frail,
The fisherman is like a fish without a tail,
The two hopeless in their future trail,
But find strength in the cant to say,
"All will be well, some day

Weeks after copulation,
There will be celebration,
Weeks after mating,
They are still dating,

She would have then conceived,
Hoping not to be deceived,
Risking her fate in another twist,
Here and now, there and in betwixt,
Bemused and confounded, she would say,
"All will be well, some day".

They gloat as custodians to the gate
And claim to hold and control our fate.
If we embrace the abundance of grace,
Earth would be a lovely and better place,
On a platter, given us on each passing day,
By Him, whose love for us will never sway,
Hence, forever I am wont to say,
"All will be well, some day"

Mission

(To the Ruler)

Mission set to make us disguise
In this melting ice,
I no more take impotent medicine
To repair my defunct menisci.

The life that I am now living,
Is why I am leaving,
A life to earn without this terror
Is better than terror without an end.

Now going the familiar paces
While watching these wringed faces,
Swirls my tepid insides and bellows
With firm overflows,
Of indelible emotions.

My chasm is not an illusion,
It heightens my fatal resignation,
To our orchestrated confusion,
Our dismembered frustration.

You as our new solution,
Morphed into the same pollution,
Mission's warped evolution,
May cause a national revulsion.

Mayhem

With the cessation of petroleum subsidy,
The veneration of this government subsides,
The scenic scenarios of yore now litter and linger,
Active reaction showcases the foreboding finger.

Bombs detonate in rolls,
Death increases in tolls,
Our weaned nation has retarded in growth,
And our lizard leaders stare and nod in tow.

Spouses lose their mates,
Lovers their loving dates,
Our destiny has become our fate,
The only life that we now may see,
Could be the encore we seek on the streets.

Vacillating in a nation whose future is so bleak,
Flashback to a cistern makes my humanity bleed,
We may resist wallowing in vengeance,
I ruminate on us and find the trajectory crazy,
And pray that our God will just show us mercy.

Ruminations

Before they dare to blow their bugle,
I would have soared like an eagle,
Far above the mounting hate and rage,
This design was inspired by my sage.

From there, I would glimpse all ethereal views,
See essential goods preceding snaking queues,
Babies stretch their hands, but are not carried,
Forcefully deflowered maidens are unmarried.

Bad choreographers prancing in fake leotards,
Rainfall cannot erase the spots of the leopard,
Carrying on with so much evil without a break,
The rat's house has been overtaken by the snake,
The rat will know no rest – nor the mice,
A wise man should never be cheated twice.

A fish out of water cannot reject help,
The fowl drinks water and raises its head,
To know from where his killers will come,
I worry about what my nation has become.
The comb knows not the hair, but the pocket,
This contraption has worn out the sprockets,
We had aimed to measure up with all the best,
But trampled, we have resorted to take a rest.

Before they dared to blow their bugle,
I would have soared like an eagle,
Far above the mounting hate and rage,
This design was inspired by my sage.

Shine Through the Gloom

Our dear ones and the people that we have lost,
Are on the other side, no more coming back to us,
Remedies are lean and lame, woven like a fable,
Though you are still strong and able.

Your followers are annoyed, sad and impatient,
Crimes are committed against all the innocent,
Give us some respite and give us a bit of grace,
We are your strength, our care will not abate.

Uncrowned delirium takes over our bastions,
Imbued with rhetoric, laced with actions,
Pushing cessation issues to the front burners,
As many of us return home as mourners.

We refresh the days we wish we never knew,
When some were Nyamiri and some Sanu,
Rodents and reptiles became our meat,
Salt was gold, plants became part of our meal,
Girls became mothers, mothers turned whores,
Nudity, scabies and kwashiorkor were norms.

Go forth to set aside these dark shadows
Threatening to take us all to the gallows,
It was your wholehearted desire to work for us,
Proceed then as a leader and try to do enough.

The gown of innocence will soon expire,
Go and conquer and remove that attire,

You will be shocked by those who retired,
Deal with this sinister air and self-denial.

Melancholy is in the land – this is our time of need,
Show them your wrath; let it befall them with speed,
They will unclench their fists, discontinue the blow,
Agree to abide by our civil rules and also kowtow,
As the tide of war recedes, change is stayed,
This would not come slowly or too late.

As you clear this room with a definite broom,
We will all bloom and shine through this gloom.

Rats

Pretend to drag the rats out of the sewers,
To save us all, the drawers and the hewers.

A shadow of sleaze still hangs around those
In cahoots with the cabal that will choose,
To weave webs with economic spiders,
To stunt our growth with subsidy wires.

They are in bed with all political scorpions,
Painting the picture of being our champions.

The Politician

It is sad,
So, so sad.

These condescending clowns,
Prancing and galloping down
An untested one-way street,
Baring a newly borne streak
That is beyond any future capture,
This enthralling alien culture,
Is ensconced in our second nature,
Searing our expected rapture.

It is sad,
So, so sad.

The Search

Show how strongly you bear
The known bestiality of your forebears,
Who smeared our graceful perch,
Entrenched in existentialist pouch,
Our beguiling hopes lie scorched.

The assumed bold president,
May not really be for all residents.

As we bolt to cast our future votes,
Zero of us knows who God bestows,
Methinks, maybe or maybe not,
Any hope? For now, a big nought.

Despair

(Black Sunday)

We now realise that nobody really cares,
Bereft of ideas, they just stand and stare,
We are now shadowy images without value,
Being walked all over in this reticent milieu.

Realise it is only bigoted mendacity you bare,
Leaving only sunlight for us to share,
The ship of state continues to sail rudderless,
We continue to grope in this abyss fatherless.

The sightless seem to grin in our silence,
Knowing our grim fate in this painful alliance,
Voyage by road is chanced by a tanker on fire,
Making your terminus an ephemeral desire.

We served too many years of ignoble sentence,
Dragged through this despair without essence,
We now laugh in sombre whispers in our parks,
As a colourless government hardly ever barks.

Mourning the manner in which they were taken,
These scenarios won't enable us to awaken,
Our destiny may be delayed, but never denied,
Cold teardrops will be harvested in time.

A domestic flight to convey you to Lagos from Abuja,
Crashes in Lagos, killing helpless scores in a déjà vu,

We mourn in the bedlam, speaking in words so soft and pure,
In this miasma of looting and darkness that we endure.

My country is a prisoner of my heart, there I sleep,
But this steep dive into a ravine makes me want to weep,
This Black Sunday leaves my soul as heavy as bricks,
As blood flows, our silent screams simmer and prick.

My mind is black, our minds blank. We sauntered home,
We only have flying coffins exhumed from distant catacombs,
A house is no more a home, as tragedy may visit you there,
Robbers, planes or tankers may whisk you from this sphere.

We keep on walking as if we are already dead,
Losing steam, we stream along with steps of lead,
Not knowing where we are going, we keep walking,
Sinking deeper into the ground and not talking.

Even if you deny all my spite, anger and pain,
Co-existing, and what do we really stand to gain?
Are we hoping through this agony for a type of bliss?
Pressed against a razor, you will not try to please.

Just trying to tour the creeks of Creek Town in peace,
I am faced with militants dumping amnesty, to secede,
We tried to please you, so that you might have a wish,
Blameful deaths drape your shoulders like a mermaid fish.

Pitch-black hair, deviant eyes firmed in beauty and majesty,
Serpentine and deceptive like the Niger-Delta Amnesty,
So much blood in your hands for what you did and didn't do,
You fabricate smiles and promises without ado.

A charade is on, with pools of blood at our soulless feet,
My saline tears cascade in symphony with our woes,
If I return to my Duke Town, I may be kidnapped by foes,
I want to be free and safe in the country of my birth,
As a glacier, a frozen territory with no boundary, but girth.

In the attics of my mind, I refuse to appreciate why the cow,
That has fed the nation is maltreated and malnourished now,
Blooming bestial pests have come home to roost,
Having failed the country, we now deserve the boot.

We Walk Among The Dead

(To the Dana Air Crash
Victims in 2012)

Mourners silently walked between rows of the dead,
Most of them fretful about their next daily bread,
153 died in a Dana airplane that was Lagos-bound,
The crash killed and maimed others on the ground.

Peering into burned faces for cognition, yet unable to tell,
Medics and onlookers wore masks to block out the smell,
"We are now without eyes, earlier this year Eke died",
Families softly wept and held each other and I also cried.

Maimuna Anyene and her family of eight with two Lebanese
Perished, along with seven Americans and four Chinese,
A Canadian and French and the Oyosoros went away,
Iniobong Nsidianabasi Asuquo's family hope is left at bay.

All is like a dream, like a drama, like a delusion,
Really burnt beyond recognition – not an illusion,
A hobbled government remains steeped in venality,
With a lax management so sure to evade penalty.

When will we transcend rhetoric and sloganeering
And reassert our goals with societal re-engineering?
"What happened to the aircraft shortly before it crashed?"
Certification by the authorities was bought with cash.

Burnt luggage and files were collected with the bodies,
While astronomers watched as Venus transited the sun,
A meteor experience due again in 105 years to come.

Rains

It is raining heavily in the midst of our pains,
The splashes of the rain on my windowpane,
Projects to me a world that is now distorted,
Portending all our plans as thwarted.

Governments will always condescend to show
Only half-truths that they want you to know,
We now see those with bulletproof masks,
Burdened deliberately to undermine the task.

Of finding real justice for all those who died,
By political masquerades with no national pride,
Previous suggested solutions met silence,
And perished due to official ambivalence.

We will do as the benevolent spirit directs,
The end is nigh in this noxious disconnect,
Motive still fails over all undisclosed details,
As a curious sense of mystery still prevails.

Let us not be overwhelmed by our scars,
And forget to continue counting our stars,
Get arrested in verse to avoid being tepid,
As we will be insulated from going putrid.

I wonder why valued bachelors and spinsters,
Have all converted into irredeemable pincers.

Jos Massacre

Death that kills a man whets an appetite,
Our women will cleanse the land,
The noonday sun,
Is the remedy for cold on a rainy day.

He that inherits his father's widow,
Will never know the high cost of marriage,
You use the finger that fits to pick the nose,
How many people will have to die
Before they know it is genocide?

A fine day makes clothes to dry in the sun,
Let our women be,
The fall of a green leaf
Is a warning to the dry ones.

The Jos Massacre is an omen
What a scene it was ... women
And their offspring in death embraces,
Huddled together in grimaces,
Departed to find some peace.
It is the death of generations, to say the least.

Our women are the mothers
Of these hoodlums and rogue boys,
The wives of heartless husbands and
Daughters of mendacious fathers of yore,
Egg was with us before the chicken,
Let our women cleanse the land.

Discordant politicians mock
The dialect of the drum
And the idiom on their lips
Is a lexicon of lies,
There is no muse in their music,
No sense beyond their sound.

Death that kills a man whets an appetite,
Our women should cleanse the land.

Tides

(Christmas Day Massacre)

Just as we hoped it would come to an end,
It started to ease and slowed to a patter,
Bombs flood home; drive us round the bend,
Pandora's Box ajar, we may begin to scatter.

On Christmas Day, the murderers came at dawn,
Treasures and cassocks amidst the trampled smell of proof,
Of evaporating tears amongst silent prayers in the calm,
Eyes viewed a dead Reverend Father on the church roof.

Once again, a memory of familiar cormorant parentage,
Shattered city ruins and distant heartbeats taken too soon,
Bonds forged in the warmth of guided historic camaraderie,
Our humanity and sprinkled compassion now disintegrates.

"It's an affront to our collective safety and freedom", Jona
    said,
Buildings are blown-up and parents killed by some insane
    people,
Even children perished, while we wish for kingdom come,
Nigeria holds a hate as this violence is no more welcome.

All these tragic events keep crawling upon us all and firmly
Cover more areas, more people killed that can be ignored,
When will the killings stop? On bended knees, we plead,
We all wish our country to have security and religious peace.

Now inundated by the Christmas catastrophic events,
Yobe, Adamawa, Plateau, Kaduna and Niger lack tenets,
The festive gathering of Christians became a milestone,
Mounds of ash and rubble forge a grindstone
To rip out her heart and bury her soul,
We teeter on the brink.

Insanity

"You must go out and kill, you must try to maim,
Never allow them to run or ever escape again."

Boko prods his clan, heads with hoods,
They were schooled in hate, right from the hood,
Religion was just for social interaction,
But society turned into spiritual desperation,
We are now facing palpable intimidation,
That requires a holistic consideration.

Then they are sated,
Because we become static,
When will they change?
When will we ever change?

There are no more safeguards in the north,
As despair resonates and springs forth,
Men of God chastise and seek protection,
They play the ostrich and reveal no real intention.

The chicken has wrongly held a grudge against the pot,
As bigots commit pogrom and still find support,
What kindness from a jihadist, you cannot see the face,
Just out-shout this mad crowd by putting on a trace.

Memory is unkind to the old, frail and graying man,
The child sees the squirrel's horns, when there is calm,
At cock-crow, only the debtor panics with fear,
The loud goatskin drum is about to tear.

Even when the wound is healed,
How will the scar tissue disappear?
Palm fruit produces oil that is red,
So does the alligator pepper.

Head hunters will never allow machete wielding
Men to stand as guards,
And no mother allows her daughter to fetch water
With a broken gourd.

The vulture that considers a bald head as an advantage will
Discover that the river that forgets its source will wilt,
In the absence of the moon, the stars will shine brightly,
If killings remain unabated, staying together is unlikely.

Then they are sated,
Because we become static,
When will they learn?
When will they ever learn?

Silence Of The Flock

Morality is doing what is right,
Regardless of what you are told,
Religion is doing what you are told,
Regardless of what is right.

The truth might always hurt,
Even to the point of breaking a heart,
But it comes with necessary pain,
Otherwise you may never gain.

The chicken survives the Christmas carnival,
Only to fatten itself for the Easter festival,
If grey hair can't find the aged to sprout on,
He grows on the young and lingers on.

The two times that
The wooden gong
Calls a mighty person in
My village, Atakpa-Ikot Efiom
Are in life and death.

Every ass loves to hear himself bray,
And the fisherwoman who for fun
Remains numb, dumb or mum,
Will never sell the wares in her tray.

Let us not disguise
In this melting ice,
That is a bugle call, folks,
In this silence... of the flock.

Edo

They acted as if they were on coke,
Posing and gallivanting with bespoke,
They were granted ample chance to rule,
But chose to inflict ten years of misrule.

The Father intervened and said it was enough,
That since their advent, things had turned tough,
In tow, the people rose up and denied them victory,
Pidipig's resurrection was then consigned to history.

The new captain, in time with the paces,
Promised not to fall through the spaces,
With the new steam, Edo will no more be bored,
As the team is working with the fear of the Lord.

Assaying

I suck up this in my strident stride
And refuse to be too contrite,
Trojan forces flank our ranks,
Dimming our lighthouse,
To hoodwink the ships at bay.

From the calm waters of the sea,
Bloated bodies were recovered,
Bodies half-eaten by the fishes,
Scarified and left on the beaches.

That baby that was eighteen inches,
Now has grown and still flinches
At the vicissitudes we will embrace,
On our defined journey to the grave.

Those who always pulverised you,
Now actually adore and idolise you,
Fight today to survive your tomorrow,
Find a place to burrow or you borrow.

Strut your stuff and let it shine,
For destiny wants you to climb.

We Return

(To the usurpers)

They gave us wine and we all made merry
And welded with grazing beasts without tokens,
Men with stoic mien were blasted and battered,
Grimaces of broken tombstones became our totems.

Remember when we were the wind when the air was still,
As the corn waited for the rains, nothing was fed to our mill.
We have all become granulated – no longer lumped,
We only say a silent prayer, readjust and attune.

Sweet and relentless songs were put to waste
By sultry and willing, but tainted saints,
We make haste,
We return.

Farmlands with floating silos called the dome,
You had purses to wreak fashion as you only played alone,
Regrets cannot atone for all the freaks in our home,
Let this temple start its transformation from stone.

We meet a desolate farmstead with a tethered bleating goat,
Through a door with a stranded doorbell yearning for repose,
Beaten warriors pray for a change in the chimes,
Our desire to assist the rebuild is real - it is time.

Sweet and relentless songs were put to waste
By sultry and willing, but tainted saints,
We make haste,
We return.

I Wish

I keep seeing the same faces
Triumphing in the same spaces,
Only adjusting different paces,
In a world contesting races.

Insolvent in simmering cases,
Dominated by a coterie of races,
I still remember these faces.

I wish,
I only wish.

Unionism

We hang out here, all of us, in the outdoors,
Weaned to forget you as neighbours,
We dare these mountains that refuse to move,
In this salient battle of ours, you may lose.

We gird our loins, anticipating your stiff scorn,
And wake to see capitulations in the morn.
Come and celebrate with our freedom song,
Reason, wisdom and justice won't be long.

Whitecap

Cleaving my heart,
To stay apart
Ever to churn,
In turn,
To the chimes,
Beats and times.

The dancers of this rhythm
On stage are strange,
Now is our time to change.

Whispers play the moving cards,
No need to split your hairs
In this game of musical chairs.

We sojourn amongst the dancers,
The drums and the masters.

My Creek Town Blues

A drowsy crocodile, a wandering piglet
And a tail-less mongrel stylise my picture,
My wife and I watching the sunset in Creek Town,
My mother's ancestral domain.

Our Obio-oko, a town located by our ancient Calabar River,
About two and a half hours from our lost Bakassi,
The Bakassi Peninsular our ancestors owned,
Melancholy was in the air,
The bitter taste was still extant over the bayou,
We were sad, very sad.

It was too early for drinking,
The weather was humid and hypnotic,
The sky on fire added to our burden,
So I walked down Mbarakom's grassy bank to a jetty
That terminated in a small thatch-roofed pavilion,
I could see the entire dark mangrove bank,
Its polished surface occasionally disturbed by
An excited fish or another prowling crocodile.

The full moon rising behind it created a garish glow
That morphed the whole scene into a painting
You could find in an art gallery in Las Vegas or
Any other sin city in the Occident or the Orient.

In the opposite direction, the over-ripe mango sun
Was descending behind a forty-story fiery form,
The shape of a serpent's head, complete with long

Luminous and vaporous tongue whipping the lush horizon,
The death glow as a postcard vista.

The incandescent beams stole our dreams
And even blocked our view of Obio Efik,
Melancholy was in the air,
The bitter taste was still extant over the bayou,
We were sad, very sad.

It was a singular sight that would cause even a sceptic
To admit at last that the degradation of our environment,
The wanton destruction of our serene habitat
And shameless flaring of our natural gas from Eket to
    Oloibiri,
Was a reality discernible all over the restive Niger Delta of
    Nigeria.

Havoc wreaked by Shell, Mobil, Chevron,
ELF, ADDAX,NNPC and their ilk,
We saw a congenial death,
Wrinkled elders got busy collecting their nets and wares,
A cue that we were running late and had to depart,
Proceeding from the monumental ruins to Calabar,
An arduous valediction to Eseku, Adak Uko, Mbarakom,
Otung,Anwa Esien Ekpe and all the bare-bodied urchins,
The nearby amiable mongrel ignored us and kept
Busy munching a raw catfish,
The scrawny cat was quietly yawning
And gnawing at an Agama lizard.

This pall of solitude attended us throughout,
From the famished streets to our Land Rover,
We drove past families all with hand-held reed torches-

Emum and old clay pot lights-Usiong, they were searching
For snails, periwinkles, edible rodents and reptiles.

We were transiting home, to our base in the capital:
To subsidy matters and subsisting strikes and boycotts,
We head back – to insecurity and spasms of government,
From Obio-oko to Obio-efik, we reached the beaches,
Where Portuguese, Spanish, German,
And the British merchant vessels once berthed,
We savour impressions of deserted dry docks,
Sea vessels we knew no longer live here.

Esuk Orok, esuk Fynn, esuk Nsidung, esuk Anantigha,
Once trading posts and natural beaches,
Have become fading impressions etched painfully in our
    history
Melancholy is in the air, apprehension is here
And fear reigns supreme,
We are sad, very sad.

Calabar

(my Hometown)

Some think that we are dated and cannot flow,
That stereotypes have got to go,
Imbibe sonorous voices and immutable rhythm,
Saintly taints our ancestors to us had given.

Calabar is clean and green, sane and tame.
And when you are done, you won't be the same.

Eternal beats, dances and communal juices,
Cascading from our mews through our sluices,
Goading your sinews to be dazed and sated,
These icebergs signpost that we are not dated.

Calabar, 'come and live and be at rest', they say,
Urban myths will remain with you when you stay,
The crocodiles' lair and mammy-water's snare,
From Hope Waddell hill, my Duke Town is clear.

Calabar is clean and green, sane and tame.
And when you are done, you won't be the same.

Crimson Ties

The urchins' disdain to be tamed
Is contagious, they now rain pain,
What was ordained, they obtain in vain,
Nobody now stands in salute to the menace,
Of those we fronted in the race for an ace.

Fraternities were in America for socialisation,
Which Nigerians imbibed for social relaxation,
And started cultivating for absolute intimidation,
Our teeming youths now join out of desperation,
Not deterred by parental and societal consideration,
This is a relapsing case which all of us now face.

Not quite long ago we stood around our parents,
Now we stand in the midst of our little children,
The sea has turned to red in town,
Listless and restless ones are in the crowd.

Death has become a matter of laughter,
As we make haste to stop the slaughter

Misguided Loss

(for Casmoke)

My eyes glistening with sad tears unshed,
As revenge goes unabated over your head,
I was angry when you ignored my warning,
My stomach churns because our town is burning.

A wife and six children now stress our friendship,
The result of cultism and abandoned internship,
Now I try to manage your self-choreographed exit,
As your hybrid won't heed advice and quit.

You guys did a detour from the queue
And I am starting to smell the stench on me,
You were murdered and dismembered,
In a way we don't want to remember.

We are pained and in communal anguish,
That your life was so brazenly extinguished,
We had always asked where you had been,
You never revealed to us that you were in.

You came from the deep valley of sacrificial lambs,
Derelicts of the society who can't have food stamps,
Yet you did some things you didn't want us to know,
And left this world at a time you didn't have to go.

Your venture amounted to a short-term gain,
This is the main reason and name of the game,

Your team, which claimed to be Robin Hood,
Capitulated and connived to rob the hood.

Anxiety does not empty tomorrow
Of all its sorrows,
It drains today of its breath
And immutable strength.

A child once bitten by a snake
Runs away from a millipede,
You feel happy when your masquerade,
Dances well in the village square,
But my masquerade that was so tame,
Exhibited banality and danced itself lame.

Peace ......On the Streets!

Killing is a game with no known title,
Only pursue your rights as is in the Bible,
You now act tough and claim not to care,
And see life as being so cruel and unfair.

I pray that we cherish our fathers' dreams,
Protecting the future from tearing at the seams,
May our leaves then blossom and bloom,
Not wither in conflating echoes of doom.

Let there be peace on our streets,
So that we can develop our place with ease
And give our people the golden chance,
In a place that kids laugh and adults can dance.

The mirth and life I crave is that of sheer fun,
Not wanton violence that makes mothers run,
With such loss of lives, we all have to bother,
So that we may still relate to one another.

We all desire a life without this pain,
Where we have more sun and less rain.
This is my inspiration and also my hope,
Life can be made better and we can cope.

Our Canaan is where the catfish meows,
The leopard struts and the sea turtle flies,
We even gave the peacock our trumpet to blow,
And resolved tiffs in Duke Town at cock-crow.

Let us drain the swamp of bitterness and hate
And erase these frowns before it gets too late,
Let God's angels continue to abide and abound,
Allowing peace to reign on the streets of my town.

Billows

At dawn, we cried out in pain,
As if beaten with a cane,
This cue makes us be brave,
Until the day we visit the grave.

That baby girl then starts to walk,
Grows on you and dons a bra,
Junior that could barely talk,
Starts to balk with a baritone.

We then prepare for our tomorrow,
While micromanaging our sorrow,
We make the best while we grow,
Life will one day stop to flow.

Your days will soon ride fast,
Making time to fly past,
Then the mirror in your own home,
Confirms the years have really flown.

When you are confronted by the dusk
For you to transform into dust,
Know that your billow has paled in peak,
Be thankful for the cusp in this beat,
It is just a homecoming to your seat.

Viktoria Duke, My Beloved Wife

When I wished for human immortality,
It was never sensed in absolute totality,
Nor envisaged to escape the sands of time,
But to forever place your hands in mine.

You are the kindest person I have ever known,
True grit and love you have always shown.
I want to give you my all, all my life,
Viktoria Duke, My Beloved Wife.

I am not fazed that as the years crawl by,
Your enchanting love continues to thrive,
Eagle-winged, we will continue to fly,
I am still your shoulder in case you want to cry.

Our sensuous bouquets of all African flowers,
Eviscerates the negative, condescending powers,
I want to give you my all, all my life,
Viktoria Duke, My Beloved Wife.

God will see us through our remaining days,
We still weather hazes that gazes our way,
Your birthday radiates the familiar feeling,
That transfigures me to a spiritual being.

Love me forever, always be by my side,
You were made to come and be my guide,
I want to give you my all, all my life,
Happy Birthday Vikki, My Beloved Wife.

My Baby

(to Viktoria Duke)

Meeting you was fate,
Transforming into your mate
Was a choice I had to take,
Falling in love was a piece of cake,
An endless feeling I could not fake.

You remain forever my special lady
Just see how far we've come, My Baby.

Viktoria Orok Duke

(My Valentine)

Though ensconced in our solitude,
We celebrate an absence of solicitude,
And are exhilarated in any Cupid beat
That renders the two of us so complete.

Valentine's is a day to say, "I love you,"
And tell you I'm happy that I have you,
This ritual is an encore to emotions real,
Exposing all that in my heart I deeply feel.

Anytime my ship sets sail in the ocean all alone,
You are the wind that brings me safely back home,
Even when darkness flickers and threatens our light,
You always make sure things remain alright.

This day of love, come love with me,
Let's sing sweet Valentine songs anew,
Love is a burden and a joy, slavery and bliss,
Being love-converts, we celebrate with a kiss.

I made a vow not to linger in the vestibule of life,
So I readily became your hubby and you my wife,
As we remain pilgrims on these earthly shores,
On St Valentine and beyond, my love is always yours.

Costa Concordia: The Sinking

They knew they were besotted, so they set sail to Italy,
The captain thought it was better to go as far as Giglio,
This sister of Costa Serena hit a rock and started swaying,
Which made all of them panic and regret ever staying.

One hundred years now, since the Titanic's hazard,
On Friday 13th, Costa Concordia faced another blizzard,
Costa Favlosa is sailing around without any worry,
Costa Pacifica is cruising and won't back down in a hurry.

To Costa Cruises in Italy, we are sad and very sorry,
Whether it is the captain or a navigational problem,
This was a ship with perfection as its emblem,
Is Concordia's fate is also tied to wicked witches of Salem?

James Thomas was not a thief and a stowaway
In the ship the day thirty-five people passed away,
He bandied his trade as a dancer in this cruise ship,
He also enjoyed its traverses in oceans deep.

The couple, copulated and then went back to sleep,
Captain Cosimo Nicastro didn't know which map to read,
They were so much in love, her voice was a generator,
It was deep, grave and sexy from her creator.

That night, the foghorn blare was far, lonely and distant,
An ocean of love had two passing ships at an equal distance,
Though they saved most crew and the passengers too,
Costa Concordia no more sails with Viktoria Duke and I.

Love Lines

Kiss, cuddle, touch and yoke me,
Or yodel loudly when caressing me,
Yesterday's gains, still imminent,
Should be made permanent.

We have to maximise these highlights,
To transport our emotions to limelight,
This love has acted now like bunting,
Still charting our solidified boundaries.

Our dreams, our wholesome dreams,
Should never again tear at the seams.
Every moment that I have spent with you,
Is like a gorgeous dream that's come true.

I find solace in the shelter of your hugs,
The home where I hone my Cupid's love bugs,
Whenever we part and other things pursue,
My mind is befuddled – I miss every inch of you.

Kiss, cuddle, touch and yoke me,
Or yodel loudly when caressing me,
Yesterday's gains are still imminent,
And should now be made permanent.

Nightmare

In the still of the night,
Under the stars bright,
With humans fast asleep,
Eka and I in passion so deep,
Shocking, inchoate and cheap.

And I'm glad I can now stay awake,
My matrimony is always at stake.

Losing Andino

This critical case
Is what we now face,
The youths think it is bravery,
Doing drugs is social slavery.

This drain on our moral treasury
Has caused communal misery,
The umbrella was for the cold weather,
Andino went bad and did not bother.

She saw no forest from the trees,
But just to satisfy her gothic needs,
Her history of wayward development,
Hatched in juvenile mismanagement.

"Guys and women all love me,
Those who don't know me still adore me".
Banal lyrics from a maniacal braggart,
Who preys on girls as his target.

J.T. lived his lyrics without muting,
Playing resurrection with his music,
Creativity in art never formed excuses,
Art against the law, not from the muses.

Though Andino always craved attention,
For her rape, J.T. should face incarceration,
Her lifestyle couldn't justify the attack,
Let us help Andino to get her life back.

The youths think it is bravery,
Doing drugs is social slavery,
This drain on our moral treasury,
Has caused communal misery.

Flourish

The portraits still flourished
When affection was famished,
Can we still feel something now,
Can we trace our way back to
These people in our pictures?

The flame we have to blame
Crawled in, unknown to our game,
Is the fire back and burning,
Or are we the ones burning?

This chosen blind alley
For us does not really tally,
Emotions too bold, yet so cold,
Flooded with no one to hold.

The portrait still flourished
When affection was famished,
Can we still feel something now,
Can we retrace our way to
These people in our pictures?

Regrets

You thought you were too blessed
To be cheated and stressed,
Now you are the one limping,
As he had you for pimping.

No more smitten, but in anger,
No more daring, you just stare:
Cursing how you fluffed it,
And carelessly lost it.

He arrived with goodies and laughter,
Then broke your heart thereafter –
Despicably cutting you up
Like you never gave each other fun.

You never saw through his schemes
That thwarted your hopes and dreams,
Now stunned and dazzled by the light,
A migrating reindeer in the night.

The caterpillar that eats the garden egg
Lives inside the garden egg,
The mistake you made, we now know,
Has turned into a communal blow

By the time he was berated,
It was already too belated.

It was a wrong turn to take,
You actually made a big mistake.

Instead of a bare knuckle fight,
Retake your life and make it right,
This shocking summer of deluge,
Has cleansed all that we begrudge.

May the early arrival of the cattle egrets,
Soothe and remind us of our sore regrets.

"Man No Rest Hotel"

Your visage betrays your mortal lust,
Your palms sweat and yearn for an encore,
The last cupid encounter was in Cally,
In a steamy area called Clerks Alley.

Carnal waves, incalescent in your groin open
A gilded chasm from the valley of your coven,
Enmeshed in the whispered mist, you void the
Foreboding churns of your enchanted dirge.

You strut, she sashays – your conquest in tow,
Past derelict spaces and terraces in Uwanse,
To rendezvous in peace in 'Man No Rest Hotel',
They warn, 'A place for relaxation, not a brothel'

Gyrating with her in the dingy, dimly lit hotel room,
Bodies on a bed, thrown in passion, curled and grovelling,
Rumpled and dirty and beddings fuming of saliva and semen,
With sweat and private fluids swaps littering the floor,
This feral bastion of fun permits a clear peek at sin,
'Man No Rest Hotel' is at your behest – it's at its peak.

Infidels

We should be discreet
And never call each other at home
And if we must call,
We must disguise our voices!

Finally, last night I dreamt of you
And the sirens said I could have you,
You are cleansed and ready for my touch,
Prepared to consummate on my couch.

This secret pact we have shared
May somehow get us ensnared.

Twisted limbs
Leave us with a limp,
Battered lips,
Conjoined at the hips,
With passion at your fingertips.

Then soft moans and cries
And loud, patronising sighs,
Your incomprehensive glance,
Taunts our cadenced dance.

I wish I knew all the days
That I would have you my way,
Our liaison acts like the phoenix,
In stolen moments that we may fix.

Lightning is the forebear of the thunder,
Your glow allows my storm to plunder,
It is like sucking nectar with every bite
And licking clementines in the night.

This secret pact we have shared
May somehow get us ensnared

Left Alone In The Past

Left alone in the past,
Friendships buried, never meant to last,
She walked away from me,
Which I couldn't foresee.

Time standing still,
A way to deal with a bitter pill,
The sky is glam with hate,
One thing tore us apart – your fate.

Now what will you do,
Who will confide in you?
Remember the times we shared,
Remember how well we paired.

The consequences are tough,
You only knew how to treat me rough,
Who is next in line,
Will you, too, break their spine?

Look at what you've done,
This time I will stand, I won't run,
Don't bother me anymore,
All that you touched, you tore.

What you wanted, you took,
Now I glance back to take one last look,
You left me alone in your past,
Friendships buried, never meant to last.

Wings

Your actions and tone of voice
Got me to doubt my choice,
We were riding the wave's crest
And geared up to be the best.

You never cared to ask me
If I boarded that London taxi,
True love will encounter banter,
That is not supposed to last.

Now the stain of this stench
Will shame and disparage us all,
Remember that Lucifer took to his trench
And ignored advice before his fall.

Termites could never decimate the bottle,
By now we should be in full throttle,
Where else would I have gone?
Sadly, I took the late train home.

At the onset I developed hesitation,
I am enveloped with resignation,
This bliss now renders a gaping gap,
Find my mast; bring your colours and tag.

We are destined for matrimony,
Harmonious, soulful symphony,
I can't play notes with broken strings,
Don't make me fly with broken wings.

Reminiscences

Sitting in my lonesome apartment in Finchley
And watching sundry, smooching squirrels swishing
Pervasively past themselves in mock dominance,
I am enthralled at their lack of human countenance.

We no longer have an abundance of these rodents
In our indeterminate homeland,
Africa can't justify the carnage,
Adults and village children of my children's age,
No longer dance and delight in this delicious pastime,
It's a pernicious gamble with a natural poisoned chalice.

I also see foxes, bush rats, rabbits, lizards and others,
So delicious, sumptuous and proteinous,
Otters, laze about in abject want for inspiration and
    excitement,
Even dreaming of becoming fully or a part of a recipe
In the waning eclectic Calabar moonlight feast.

Africa has also lost interest in destroying and
Consuming its natural game,
Reality bites, as I retract and saunter away,
From the desolate window pane.

Don't Judge Me

Don't judge me in the past,
I don't live there anymore,
The only thing you may see,
Is what the fire left behind,
I have my memories unkind.

What the caterpillar sees as
The end is what wise men
Call a beautiful butterfly,
Love is just a word until
Somebody comes along to
Give it a real meaning, too.

It might be stormy now,
But it cannot rain forever in tow,
The mercury rose and records fell,
Our windy weather changed and hellish
Storms ravaged our homely homes,
And infernos fraught the Atlantic coast
To weeping icicles and melting ice caps.

We do not really feel hopeless,
Rising sea levels scare us so silly,
We rise and rinse like the wren
Knowing that we are waited for,
Our lavish daily meals are free
With no contributions or a fee,
Savings or money as part of the deal.

Everybody seems to have an opinion now,
Ready to kick you when you are down,
Let actions be taken until we are done,
Wait no more for none cares to come,
Passion declined when hope was gone.

Judge me not in the past you recall,
I no longer pay it homage at all.

Idim Uyo

(Uyo Stream)

This outing of ours in the ravine had a purpose;
Left in the lone boat, swinging about at will in the current,
In the middle of the current, my trashing around and
    infantile
Fidgeting became an overdue freedom for the canoe and I.

Momentarily, I was free and floating away, lying face up,
Besotted by that feeling you love, and love not to be named.

I was the prince, greeted by the grasses by the banks,
And the trees whispered to the breezes their consent.
    It was
So pleasant, I lost all worldly cares, oblivious of the
    snakes,
From my forlorn abode, I heard the commotion.

Faint cacophony of earthly sounds was prodding my peace,
Then I crashed into another boat and jolted awake,
To realize that the truncation of my journey was
Human motivated. Mean faces barking and sniping
At me for trying to kill myself. "Don't you know
That this stream flows to Ifiayong Obot Utai?"
"What would we have told mummy?" they yelped.

My reaction and succour were frozen and stored
To be relived at a later date,
In silence, I grieved and crawled out of the canoe,

Picked my water gourd by the bank,
Collected the volume of water that my little head
Could endure and my diminutive legs could tolerate and
Could carry up the undulating hills of the decanting
   Idim Uyo -
The new recourse,
The resource

Uyo

(the Thread)

Whisper not to me of the great Uyo circus
Or that ageless warrior in history's span,
Idim Uyo's grim beach, sands and mean geckos,
Fallen houses where Eka Street stands.

Remember, there is no eternal hour with power,
Tarry and believe and smell like the rose flower.

I heard of practising school for the moulding of dreams,
Of a fairyland and TTC, Uyo was home to virgin realms,
UPE, Afia Eto competed with CKS, Barracks Road for a
    piece,
In this land of sweet delight and patriotism by a precipice.

Supporting Nigeria in the strife was a fair and noble cause,
Saboteurs' honour and deceit was paid for without pause,
Ikot Ekpene was won and lost, severally without reclaim,
Capt. Gagara died and Udo Ekpa died without worldly
    gain.

JJ Okon, Ating were heads. Obot and Umanah were also
    there,
My family, the clan and relief goods were the essential
    thread,
This spirit bound our comradeship and our sultry travails,
In Uyo, we baited the liberation with nocturnal rallies.

Continue with your adamant and incisive repudiation,
Clothed in denial and personal contamination,
Scepticism in the abundance of data and future implication?
Anwanga-Abasi and the patriots went against irate
desperation.

Remember, there is no eternal hour with power,
Tarry and believe and smell like the rose flower.

Death of Ete'Kamba

(For Muamar Ghaddafi: 1942-2011)

He promised to die "on our African soil"
And decidedly appeased the ephemeral toil,
Our piper played the solemn note to herald
The end of an epoch and era,
Needless lament for one of the best,
Loftily, he simply went home to rest.

Arabs need not cry farewell to him,
Bruised and broken, no token of
Your love will not suffice thereof,
Or redeem your cause from the grave,
Hang your bestial heads in shame,
His fame and name,you could not tame.
Sahel's dream is gone,Ete'kamba is slain.

You couldn't face the man in life,
But smeared his gain in the afterlife,
He sought to free Africa at last,
Now that he is gone,free the birds of war,
They can follow now without the songs,
Africa is on rampage to kill all her sons.

Africa

(in the aftermath)

Now that their future has become futile,
The dead weights no longer see the deadline,
We celebrate our collective amnesia in droves,
Our primeval instincts in our feral coves.

"Please, celebrate me home," the soloist sang,
Africa will still sway, to the song of the gang,
In the aftermath
Of the bloodbath.

Now distinct in scripted scenes from beyond
Our decadent shores, as foretold by Biko andthers.
"Africa kills her children", Saro-Wiwa said,
Moulded heroes and sheroes who left our stead.

"Please, celebrate me home", the soloist sang.
Africa will still sway, to the song of the gang.
In the aftermath
Of the bloodbath

Angst

(Invasion of Africa)

These sanguinarians bleat and
Tactfully, down they beat
Your mind, body and bones,
Then they return to their homes.

I am not assigned to pretend,
With such sinews to contend,
My motion is rooted in our riposte,
Crafted by their bold pirates of old.

The scramble has again begun,
We are sequestered. Don't recant.

We cannot celebrate,
Or by any reason accentuate
The visits of your chameleons,
Nor your evolving schemes.
We were succulent, nay,
Bitterly truculent at bay.

My notion footed to inspire
Those who don't even perspire,
The beast latches on and salivates,
Sneers and also belly-aches
When others fill the empty space

And so the pattern replays again,
Ingratiating a negative refrain.

These sanguinarians bleat and
Slowly down they beat
Your mind, body and bones,
Then return home to their clones.

Mummy Dearest

(Elder Amayo Edet Duke:1930-1996)

You are not dead,
You left a great heritage of joy,
She still lives in our hearts,
In the happiness we knew-our woman of Troy.

She still breathes,
In the dreams we shared,
In the lingering fragrance,
From her favourite flowers,

She still smiles under our moonlight
And laughs in our sunlight's sparking gold.

She still speaks,
In the echoes of the words that I had
Heard her teach again and again.

She still moves,
In the rhythm of waving grasses,
In the dance of the tossing branches.

Mummy is not dead,
Her memory is warm in our hearts,
Though we seek comfort in our sorrow,
She is not apart from us, but a part of us.

For my love for you is eternal,
You shall be with us as a mother
Throughout all eternity,
She ...is not dead.

Eteyen, My Brother(Edem Otu Duke:1958-1981)

Wherever you are, Edem,
May you find comfort there,
In the arms of the angels.

That week you had hoped to watch
An inter-continental wrestling match,
Mighty Igor was in Calabar town
With cronies, buddies and clowns,
You vowed to watch, we all agreed,
But that week you left, at nearly twenty-three.

February, 1981, Edem you left me at your place,
You gave up the ghost and the earthly race,
Evergreen, your memory will always be,
You bestowed hope and gave me the key,
Eteyeneka, stay on, for we will again meet.

Wherever you are, Edem,
May you find comfort there,
In the arms of the angels.

O! the pangs and the pain
Have given us no rest or gain,
I had also, become much as tame,
As the way you played the game.

Am still here with Vickie and the kids
I wish you had, alas, no known kids.

Wherever you are, Edem,
May you find comfort there,
In the arms of the angels.

Lightning Source UK Ltd.
Milton Keynes UK
UKHW022238300621
386426UK00002B/39

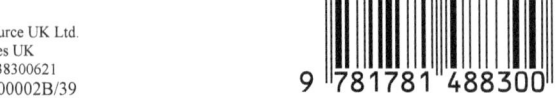